Sew in *Style*

Make Your Own Doll Clothes

22 Projects for 18˝ Dolls
Build Your Sewing Skills

Erin Hentzel

FunStitch
STUDIO
stitch your art out.

Publisher: Amy Marson

Creative Director: Gailen Runge

Art Director: Kristy Zacharias

Editors: Liz Aneloski and Lee Jonsson

Technical Editors: Susan Hendrickson and Alison M. Schmidt

Cover/Book Designer: April Mostek

Production Coordinator: Jenny Davis

Production Editor: Joanna Burgarino

Illustrator: Jenny Davis

Photo Assistant: Mary Peyton Peppo

Photography by Diane Pedersen and Nissa Brehmer of C&T Publishing, Inc., unless otherwise noted

Published by FunStitch Studio, an imprint of C&T Publishing, Inc., P.O. Box 1456, Lafayette, CA 94549

Library of Congress Cataloging-in-Publication Data

Hentzel, Erin, 1966-

 Sew in style : make your own doll clothes : 22 projects for 18-inch dolls : build your sewing skills / Erin Hentzel.

    pages cm

 ISBN 978-1-60705-795-6 (soft cover)

 1. Doll clothes--Patterns. I. Title.

 TT175.7.H47 2014

 745.592'21--dc23

                    2013033260

Printed in China

10 9 8 7 6 5 4 3 2

dedication

To Avery and her dolls, for their patience during the many hours of modeling and pattern testing

acknowledgments

Writing this book was fun and a lot of work. It would not have been possible without help and encouragement from others.

I would like to thank everyone from C&T Publishing who worked hard to make my book amazing, especially Roxane and Liz, who answered my numerous questions through this very cool adventure. Many thanks to Jamie from Dear Stella fabrics and Demetria from RJR Fabrics; their fabrics were wonderful to work with and absolutely perfect for doll clothes. Thank you to Jackie from Havel's Sewing, whose knowledge was tremendously helpful in finding the ideal scissors for kids.

A very special thank-you to my family, who sometimes had to pitch in when Mom was busy playing with her dolls.

contents

 *Sewing level (see page 7)*

introduction
How to Use This Book

The Go-To Chapter

Chapter 1 is The Go-To Chapter. It tells you about the basic supplies and sewing tools you'll need. It shows you how to sew with a sewing machine and by hand. It tells you a bit about different types of fabric and what machine needle to use when sewing those fabrics. It is filled with photo tutorials and sewing help. Go to this chapter to see how things are done or for extra help when sewing a project.

The Projects

Use the patterns on the pullout pattern sheets to cut out your fabric pieces. Some projects call for fabric pieces that are rectangles. For these pieces, you will use a ruler and fabric marker to draw cutting lines and then cut those pieces out of your fabric.

Each set of pattern instructions includes a list of supplies, in addition to your sewing basket supplies, that you need to make that particular project. When projects in the book are designed for woven fabric, the instructions will say "fabric" in the supply list. When projects are designed for knit fabric, the instructions will say "knit fabric" in the supply list.

More about the Projects

Each project has step-by-step photos to help you sew the project. Many of the projects have you do the same steps. Instead of repeating these instructions, a page number will be given for you to find more help with that step.

The Sewing Levels

You will see the recommended sewing level for each project under the project title and in the Table of Contents. This will help you choose a project that is right for your sewing ability. Begin with sewing levels ✳ and ✳½ if you are just starting out. Sewing these level ✳ projects over and over will help you to get better at sewing with a seam allowance and will help you get ready to sew the level ✳✳ projects. Before moving on to level ✳✳ and ✳✳✳ projects, make sure you can accurately sew straight and curved seams with a ¼" seam allowance. After you've sewn several level ✳ projects and are feeling comfortable with those projects, move to a level ✳✳.

Level ✳
beginner projects

Level ✳✳
advanced beginner projects

Level ✳✳✳
intermediate projects

You Be the Designer!

In the Final Thoughts chapter (page 110), you'll find some ideas and inspiration for how to add special details to all your projects. This section is great when you are ready to be your doll's designer and create several different looks with the same pattern.

A Few Things to Remember

Whenever you try new things, you will make mistakes. This is good, because it means you're also learning. The more you sew, the better you'll get, so keep sewing and trying new things. No one's sewing is perfect. My sewing certainly isn't, and I've been sewing for more than 35 years. That's okay. Sewing and creating is fun; it's not about being perfect. Go slowly and do each step carefully before moving on to the next step.

The Go-To Chapter

This is the chapter to go to for help.

What's in This Chapter?

Your Sewing Basket

You'll need some supplies and common sewing tools. A shoe box, plastic container, or basket can be a great place to keep all your sewing supplies. Your sewing basket can be anything you want it to be.

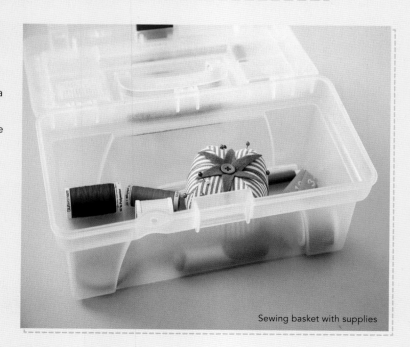

Sewing basket with supplies

Here is a list of things you'll want to keep in your sewing basket and that you will need to sew the projects in this book.

A **Hand sewing needles.** I use embroidery needles for hand sewing. They have sharp points and big eyes for easy threading.

B **A place to store your sewing needles.** A piece of felt, felt needle book, or wooden needle box all work great.

C **Needle threader.** This handy gadget helps you thread your needle quickly when hand sewing.

D **Fabric scissors.** A good pair of sharp scissors will save you time and frustration when cutting your patterns out of fabric.

tip
Keep your fabric scissors sharp. Only cut fabric, thread, and ribbon with them.

E **Spools of thread.** All-purpose thread is best for the projects in this book. Choose thread that matches your fabric.

F **Straight pins.** Use straight pins for pinning patterns to the fabric and for pinning fabric together before you sew a seam.

G **Pincushion.** A pincushion is a place to put your pins. It is easier to grab a pin from a pincushion than from a flat surface when you're sewing.

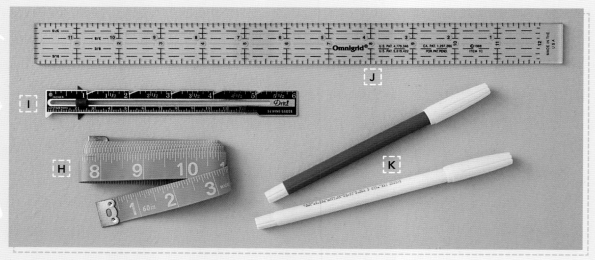

H **Measuring tape.** Since it's flexible, it's perfect for measuring things that are round or curved, like your doll's waist.

I **Sewing gauge.** A sewing gauge helps you mark stitching lines and pressing folds. You can use the blue slider to set it to your desired seam allowance or to the length you need to fold.

tip
On the sewing gauge, an inch is divided into 8 equal parts, so the second line equals ¼˝.

J **Ruler.** Use a ruler for drawing the cutting lines on some of the book's projects.

K **Fabric marker or tailor's chalk.** This is useful for drawing cutting lines directly onto fabric and for transferring pattern markings onto your fabric.

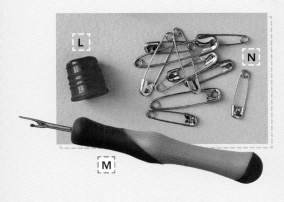

L **Thimble.** When hand sewing, place the thimble on your middle finger to protect it from getting poked when pushing the needle through your fabric.

M **Seam ripper.** This tool helps you pick out stitches when you make a mistake. And we all make mistakes.

N **Safety pins.** Use safety pins when inserting elastic or drawstrings into casings.

In addition to your sewing basket, keep an iron and ironing board handy. If you don't have these available, no worries! You can still make all the projects without them.

More Helpful Tools

As you sew more and more, you may want to gradually collect additional sewing tools to help you with your sewing projects. These tools are designed to make sewing easier but are not absolutely necessary.

O **A ¼″ presser foot.** This makes sewing a ¼″ seam allowance much easier. Using a ¼″ presser foot means that if you sew with the edge of your presser foot lined up with the edge of your fabric, you will be sewing a ¼″ seam allowance.

P **Pinking shears.** The zigzag blades are designed for fabric. Pinking shears are the easiest way to finish seam allowances.

Q **Small, sharp scissors.** These are great for cutting threads and clipping curves.

R **Dritz Ezy-Hem.** This is good for folding and pressing hems and casings.

S **A corner-turning tool.** This helps you poke out corners after turning a project right side out. Some have a flat edge for "finger-pressing."

A Little about Fabrics

Woven Fabrics

Woven fabrics don't have much stretch when you tug on them. When project instructions call for woven fabrics, look for fabrics such as quilting cotton, calico cotton, chambray, lightweight denim, flannel, poplin, or corduroy.

Knit Fabrics

Knit fabrics are stretchy. T-shirts are made from knit fabrics. When project instructions call for knit fabrics, look for fabrics such as cotton Lycra, jersey knit, and cotton interlock. Because knit fabrics don't unravel, there is no need to finish the seam allowances of knits.

Selvage

Fabric has a width and a length. The selvage edge is the length. It sometimes has writing on it. The width of fabric is the other direction, perpendicular to the selvage edge. Be sure to cut off the selvage edge before pinning and cutting pattern pieces.

tip

Most projects use small pieces of fabric. Use scraps you have on hand. And check the remnant bin at your local fabric store.

Width of fabric

Selvage

Length of fabric

Fabric Print and Scale

The design printed onto the fabric is sometimes called the print. The scale is how large or small the design is.

tip

When making doll clothes, you may want to choose smaller-scale prints. These smaller-scale prints look great on doll clothes, and the design of a large-scale print might be lost when you cut out your pattern pieces. Narrow lace and ribbons also work well for embellishing your doll's outfits and accessories. You should choose what you like ... large-, medium-, or small-scale prints ... you are the designer. Whatever you choose, your doll will like too.

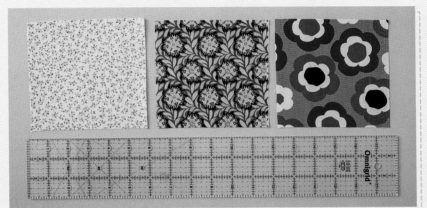

From left to right: small-scale print, medium-scale print, large-scale print

Think about Direction

Look carefully at the direction of the design on your fabric before you cut out your pattern pieces. You don't want to accidentally sew something with the picture upside down. Here are some examples.

tip

When your fabric has a specific direction to its design, make sure all the pattern pieces are facing the same way.

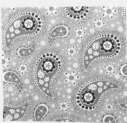

The fabric in the upper left corner is the only one that would need all the pieces cut in the same direction.

Using a Pattern

Cutting Out Paper Patterns

The first step to sewing doll clothes is to find each of the pattern pieces listed in the project's supply list. Use craft scissors (not your fabric scissors) to carefully cut around the paper pattern pieces to separate them. Each pattern piece is labeled with the name of the project, what part of the project it is (sleeve, front, back, etc.), and how many fabric pieces to cut from the pattern.

The outside solid lines are the cutting lines, and the dashed lines are the sewing lines.

What's on a pattern?

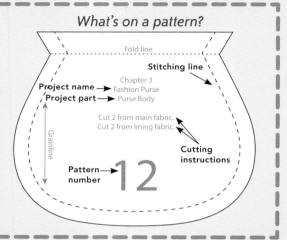

Fold line

Stitching line

Project name → Chapter 3
Fashion Purse

Project part → Purse Body

Cut 2 from main fabric.
Cut 2 from lining fabric.

Cutting instructions

Grainline

Pattern number → 12

tip

To make your patterns last longer, trace the paper patterns onto tracing paper or pattern-tracing fabric. Use the tracings to cut out the fabric pieces. Fold the paper patterns neatly and store them in a plastic bag or manila envelope when you are finished with the project.

Grainline

Some pattern pieces will have the grainline marked. The grainline should be placed straight on the grain of the fabric. Here's how to do that.

Place this line parallel to the selvage edge of the fabric. Use a ruler to measure both ends of the grainline to make sure it is straight and parallel to selvage edge.

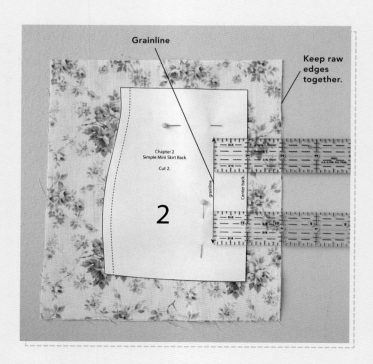

Grainline

Keep raw edges together.

Chapter 2
Simple Mini Skirt Back

Cut 2.

2

Pinning the Pattern Pieces to the Fabric and Cutting Them Out

Use straight pins to pin the pattern pieces onto the fabric. Pins should be placed inside and parallel to the cutting lines, poked through the pattern and all layers of fabric. Once the pattern piece is pinned all the way around, cut around the pattern piece along the solid cutting lines.

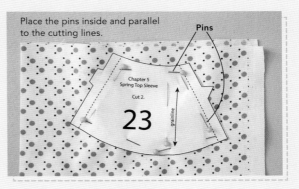

Place the pins inside and parallel to the cutting lines.

Pins

Chapter 5
Spring Top Sleeve

Cut 2.

23

grainline

tip

Make sure to move pins out of the way when cutting out your fabric. You can damage your scissors by cutting into a pin.

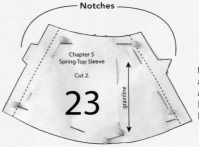

Notches

Chapter 5
Spring Top Sleeve

Cut 2.

23

grainline

Make sure to cut around the notches along the cutting lines. These are helpful markings.

Cutting Out 1 Pattern Piece

When the pattern piece says "Cut 1," pin the pattern piece to a single layer of fabric and cut on the solid cutting lines.

Cutting Out 1 Pattern Piece on the Fold

Fold your fabric in half, with selvage edges even. Place the fold line of the pattern along the folded edge of the fabric and pin it there. Then pin the rest of the pattern onto the fabric. Cut around the pattern piece through both layers of fabric, but *don't* cut along the fold line.

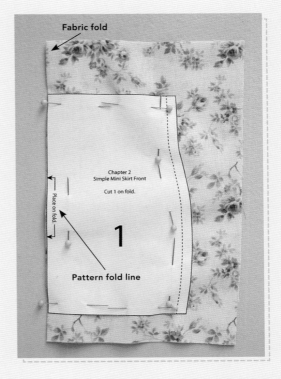

Fabric fold

Chapter 2
Simple Mini Skirt Front

Cut 1 on fold.

Place on fold

1

Pattern fold line

Cutting Out 2 Pattern Pieces

When the pattern piece says "Cut 2," fold the fabric in half, with the selvage or raw edges even. If you are using 2 separate pieces of fabric, make sure to place the fabric wrong sides together.

Or, you can use pinking shears to cut the patterns out of the fabric. Just make sure not to cut into the cutting line.

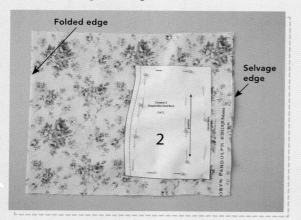

Cutting Fabric Pieces without Patterns

When a piece included in the pattern is a square or rectangle, you will use the measurements given instead of a paper pattern. Place your fabric with the wrong side facing up. When you need to cut out 2 pieces, fold your fabric with right sides together and use straight pins to keep your fabric together while cutting the pieces out.

step 1

Use a ruler and fabric marker to draw the cutting lines according to the measurements given in the project instructions.

step 2

Cut along the lines you've drawn.

Sewing by Hand

First, you'll need to thread your needle and make a knot at the end of your thread. Cut about an arm's length of thread. Make a loop near an end and pass the tail through the loop 1 to 3 times, then pull tight. The more times you put the tail through the loop, the bigger the knot will be.

When sewing by hand, hold the needle at the eye, keeping the thread between your finger and thumb. This will help keep your needle from coming unthreaded while you sew.

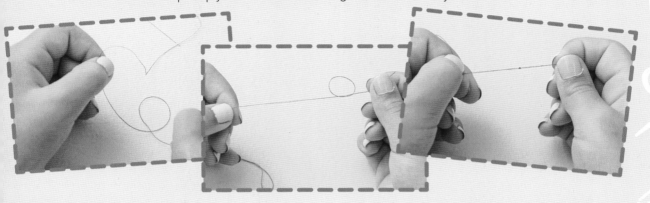

Securing Your Stitches

Sew a little x at the beginning and end of your stitching line. Do this inside the seam allowance. This step will help prevent your stitches from coming out later.

When you are finished sewing a seam, tie a knot in your thread close to the fabric. Trim any extra thread.

note

I used contrasting thread in the photos to show the stitching. For your projects, choose thread that matches your fabric.

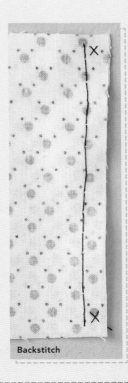

Backstitch

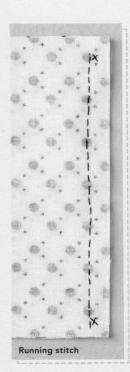

Running stitch

The Running Stitch (Also Known as the Straight Stitch)

The running stitch is a straight stitch you can use for seams and hems.
It looks like a dashed line when sewn.

step 1

Pull the needle up from the back side about ¼″ in from the side edge.

step 2

Poke the needle back down through the fabric a little way to the left of where it came up.

step 3

Pull the needle up to the front of the fabric the same amount of space to the left.

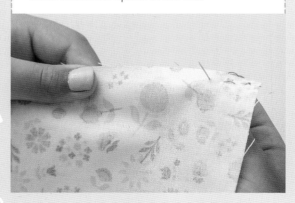

step 4

Repeat.
You can also make several stitches at once.

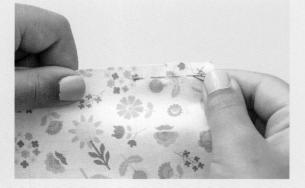

The Backstitch

The backstitch is another straight stitch that can be used for seams. Sew right to left across the fabric.

step 1

Pull the needle up from the back side about ¼″ in from the side edge.

step 2

Poke the needle down through the fabric a bit to the right of where the needle came up through the fabric.

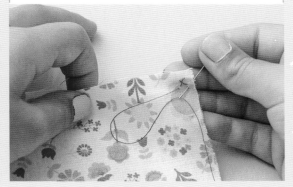

step 3

Pull the needle up from the back, so it comes up a little to the left of the last stitch.

step 4

Poke the needle down through the fabric at the edge of the last stitch (the point where the needle first came up in Step 1).

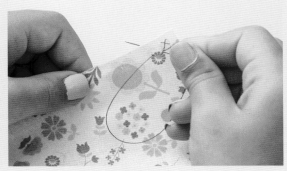

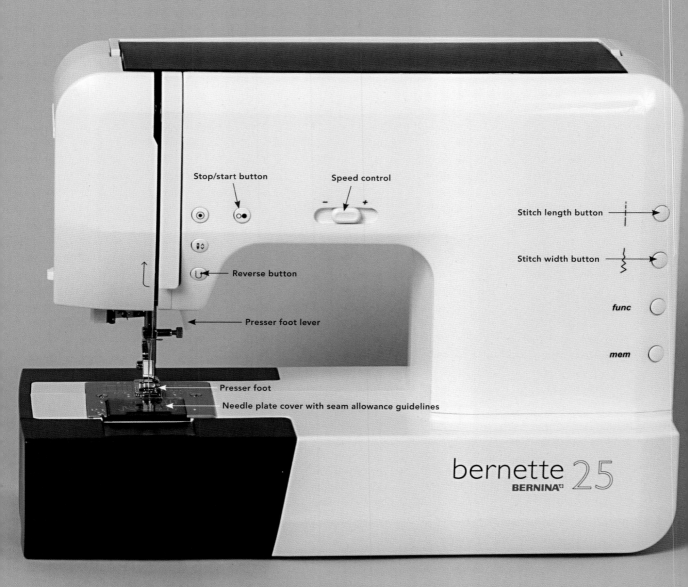

Stop/start button

Speed control

Stitch length button

Stitch width button

func

mem

Reverse button

Presser foot lever

Presser foot

Needle plate cover with seam allowance guidelines

bernette 25
BERNINA

Sewing by Machine

If you are pretty new to sewing on a sewing machine, practice sewing on paper. Take the thread and bobbin out of your machine and sew on paper to get used to guiding the paper as you sew, controlling your speed, and sewing straight and curved lines.

Begin by drawing some straight lines and some wavy lines on paper. First sew on the straight lines. Then, sew along the wavy lines. Next, draw simple shapes on paper and practice sewing on those lines.

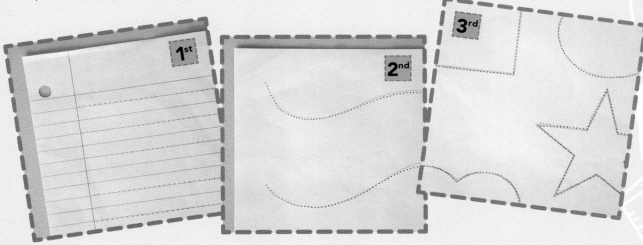

To practice sewing with a seam allowance, draw some simple shapes (still working on paper), and mark a dashed stitching line ¼″ from the outer edge.

Cut the shapes out and practice sewing on the dashed line.

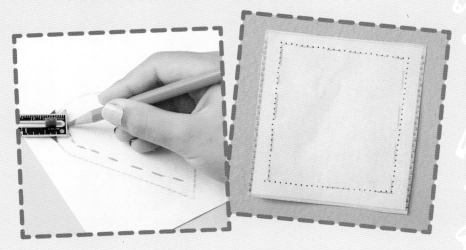

Sewing Machine Needles

You can use different needles in your sewing machine depending on the material you are sewing.

 **Universal:** Use for sewing quilting cottons, calicos, chambray, and seersucker.

 **Stretch:** Use for fabrics with stretch, like cotton Lycra and spandex.

 Microtex: Use for sewing finer fabrics, like poplin and satin.

 Jeans/Denim: Use for thick woven fabrics, like denim, corduroy, and canvas.

 Jersey/Ball Point: Use for sewing knits without a lot of stretch, like cotton interlock.

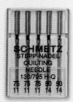 **Quilting:** Use for sewing multiple layers of fabric with batting, like the sleeping bag project.

Choose the right machine needle for your fabric.

Sewing Seams

Pinning the fabric together helps keep the layers of fabric from shifting while you sew. Place the fabric pieces together, matching up all the edges. Place the pins perpendicular to the stitching line that you are planning to sew.

 tip

When sewing your seams, stop and remove each pin as it gets close to the presser foot. *Do not sew over pins.* Sewing over pins can make your stitches go wonky. Or worse, you could break a pin or needle and damage your machine.

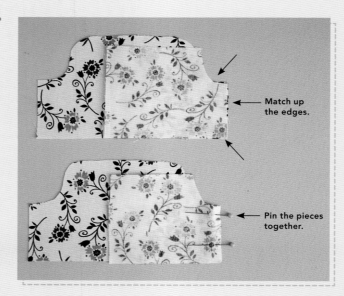

Match up the edges.

Pin the pieces together.

A seam allowance is the distance from your stitching line to the raw edge. Most sewing machines have lines next to the presser foot to help you sew a specific seam allowance width. Keeping the edge of the fabric lined up with one of these lines helps you sew a straight seam with a specific seam allowance.

tip

You may find it helpful to place a piece of colored tape along the seam allowance line on the sewing machine. This helps you see the seam allowance line clearly as you sew, making it easier to guide the edge of the fabric along the desired seam allowance line.

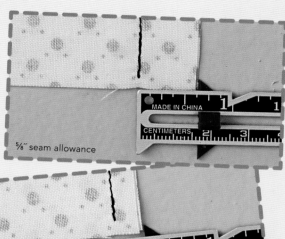

⅝" seam allowance

¼" seam allowance

When sewing woven cotton fabric, use a straight stitch.

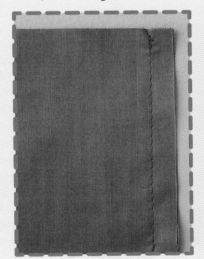

When sewing knit fabrics, use a narrow zigzag stitch.

This is a wide zigzag stitch.

tip

When you take your project out of your sewing machine, make sure to leave the top thread about 3" or 4" long. This stops the needle from coming unthreaded when you start sewing again.

- Use pinking shears when cutting the pattern pieces out of fabric. (See page 16.)

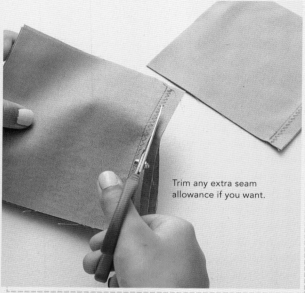

Trim any extra seam allowance if you want.

- Sew zigzag stitches within the seam allowances after sewing a seam. Sew through both layers and be careful to not sew over the seam (the straight stitches). Do this before moving on to the next step in your sewing project.

- Trim seam allowances with pinking shears after sewing a seam.

Securing Your Stitches

When sewing a seam, you will want to keep the stitches from coming out. Secure the stitches at the beginning and end of your stitching line.

step 1

Sew 3 or 4 stitches forward.

step 2

Stop and sew 3 or 4 stitches backward right on top of the stitches you've just sewn.

step 3

Continue sewing forward.

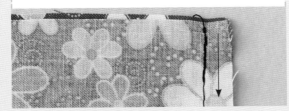

tip

Sewing machines have a reverse lever or button. Press and hold this down to sew backward.

Do the same at the end of the seam. When you reach the end of where you need to sew (Step 1), stop, sew 3 or 4 stitches backward (Step 2), stop, and sew 3 to 4 stitches forward again (Step 3).

step 1

Stop sewing when you reach the end.

step 2

Sew 3 or 4 stitches backward, right on top of the stitches you've just sewn.

step 3

Sew 3 or 4 stitches forward.

tip

Trim all threads close to the fabric after sewing each step. This makes your project easier to work with and helps your project look its best.

Pressing Seam Allowances

Depending on the project, you will press the seam open or to the side.

Seam allowances pressed open

Seam allowances pressed toward the side

If you have finished your seam allowances after sewing a seam, you will need to press the seam allowances to the side.

Finger-Pressing

To finger-press means to make creases and folds in the fabric with your fingers instead of with an iron. With the fabric between your forefinger and thumb, run your thumb or thumbnail over the folded edge to press a crease along the fabric.

You can also place the fabric on a hard surface and run your thumb across the fold in the fabric.

Making a Double-Folded Hem

Fold the fabric ¼″ toward the wrong side. Press with an iron.

tip
When folding and ironing hems and casings, use a sewing gauge or the Dritz Ezy-Hem to make sure you're pressing evenly and accurately across the fabric.

step 2

Fold again and press. For a ½″ hem allowance, the second fold will measure ¼″.

For a ⅝″ hem allowance, the second fold will measure ⅜″.

step 3

Sew across the fabric, close to the inside fold.

Inside fold

Sewing a Casing for an Elastic Waistband or Drawstring

step 1

Work with the project inside out; fold the fabric ¼″ toward the wrong side of the fabric and press with an iron.

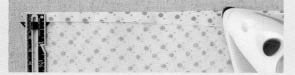

step 2

Fold the fabric edge again ½″ toward the inside of the project and press.

step 3

Pin in place and sew around, close to the inside folded edge, to make a casing (or tunnel) for the elastic or drawstring. If your project is sewn into a loop, like pants or shorts, leave 1½″ to 2″ unsewn. This opening is where you will insert the elastic or drawstring.

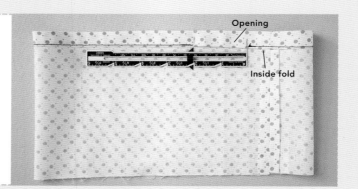

Opening

Inside fold

Inserting the Elastic

step 1

Attach a safety pin to an end of the elastic or drawstring. Insert the safety pin into the opening of the casing.

step 2

Push and scrunch the fabric with 1 hand as you push the safety pin farther into the casing.

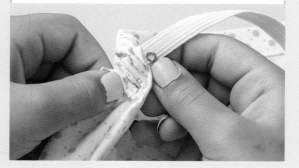

tip

Placing a safety pin on both ends of your elastic keeps you from losing the tail inside the casing and having to start over.

step 3

Hold on to the safety pin with 1 hand and smooth out the fabric with the other hand, releasing the gathers.

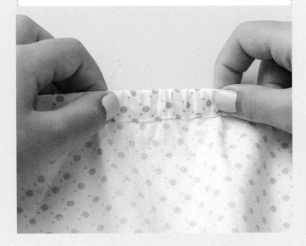

step 4

Feed and work the safety pin and elastic in this way, all the way around the casing, until the safety pin comes out the other end.

Make sure to watch the back end of the elastic and don't let it go into the casing as you work the elastic around the casing. If it looks like it might disappear into the casing, use a straight pin to hold it in place at the opening (or put another safety pin on the tail end).

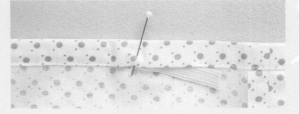

step 5

Once the safety pin comes out the other side of the opening in the casing, pull both ends of the elastic to give yourself enough elastic to work with, and pin the 2 ends of the elastic together. Overlap the ends a bit (¼˝ or so) and sew the 2 ends together, making sure the elastic is not twisted.

Sew a box shape using a straight stitch. Or …

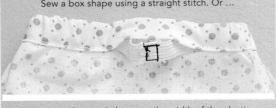

… use a zigzag stitch across the width of the elastic.

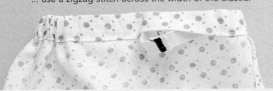

step 6

Use your hands to stretch the waist of the project open, so that the elastic goes back into the casing all the way. Sew the opening closed with a straight stitch.

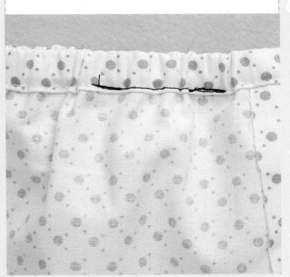

Sewing and Trimming Corners

When sewing corners, you'll need to pivot. Here's how.

step 1

Mark your stitching lines along the seam allowance.

When you reach the corners, make a dot where the 2 stitching lines meet.

These dots are your pivot points.

step 2

Begin sewing, using a straight stitch. When you reach the dot at the corner, stop and put the needle down into the fabric on the dot by turning the handwheel toward you.

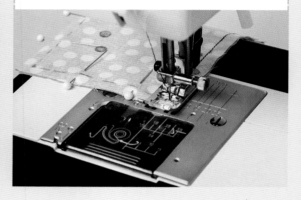

step 3

Lift the presser foot and turn the fabric to turn the corner.

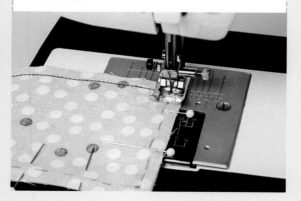

step 4

Lower the presser foot and sew the next side.

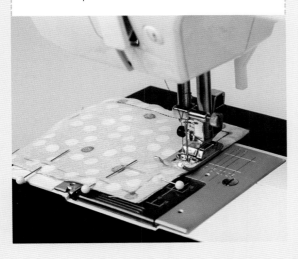

step 5

Cut diagonally across the seam allowances at the corner, but do not cut the stitches.

step 6

Then trim along the sides, right next to the corner.

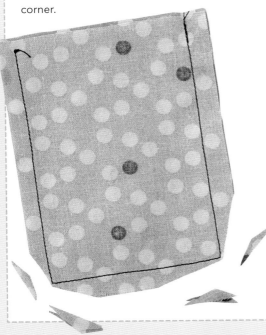

step 7

Turn the piece right side out. You can use a corner-turning tool to poke out the corners. Just be careful not to poke through the stitches and make a hole in your project.

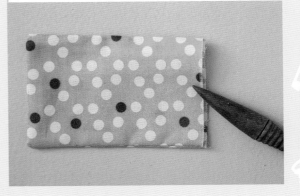

Sewing and Clipping Curves ---------------

When sewing a curved edge, use a short stitch length and sew slowly. Stop every 2 or 3 stitches with the needle down in the fabric, lift the presser foot, and adjust the fabric to keep on the curve (just like when you pivot, but turn the fabric just a little). Make sure to lower the presser foot before sewing again.

It can also be helpful to mark your stitching lines along a curve before sewing.

tip

When sewing curved or rounded edges—

- Draw the stitching line.
- Sew slowly.
- Use a shorter stitch length (2–2.5 on most sewing machines).
- Stop often and adjust the fabric.

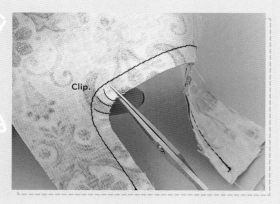

Clip.

After you've sewn an inside curved edge, you'll need to clip the seam allowance along the curve. To clip curves, make little cuts with scissors up to stitching line. Be very careful not to cut the stitches. Here is an inside curve sewn and clipped.

For outside curves, cut little triangles out of the seam allowance. Be very careful not to cut the stitches.

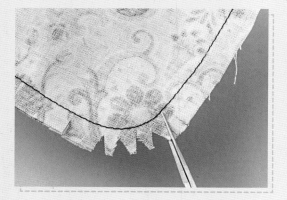

Sewing Hook-and-Loop Tape

Many of the doll clothes in this book have an opening in the back. To keep the clothes on, you will need to attach hook-and-loop tape. Hook-and-loop tape has 2 parts: a scratchy, stiff side (hooks) and a fuzzy, soft side (loops). When they meet, they stick together.

tip

Hook-and-loop tape can be cut narrower to make the clothes less bulky. Use the part you trim off for your next project! You can also cut the scratchy side a little narrower than the soft side to prevent your doll's hair from getting caught in it.

step 1

With the hook-and-loop tape stuck together, cut a piece to fit the back opening of your project.

step 2

Fold and iron a side of the center back opening ½″ toward the inside. Leave the other side of the center back opening unfolded.

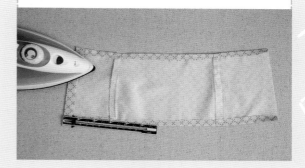

tip

Because all 18″ dolls are not exactly the same size, most of the projects have an open-back design that can be adjusted slightly to better fit your doll. Check to see how the clothing fits your doll before sewing the hook-and-loop tape on so you can make it fit tighter or looser.

step 3

Sew around all 4 sides of the soft side of the hook-and-loop tape, attaching it to the folded side of the center back.

step 4

Sew around all 4 sides of the scratchy side of the hook-and-loop tape, attaching it to the unfolded side of the center back opening, placing it on the right side of the fabric.

step 5

After sewing both pieces of the hook-and-loop tape to the center back opening, it should look like the photo below on the outside when fastened.

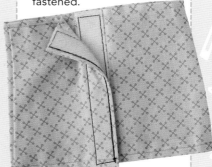

tip

You can use a zigzag stitch or a straight stitch to sew the hook-and-loop tape to your doll clothes.

glossary
What Does That Word Mean?

Baste (or basting stitch)

A long, straight stitch used to keep fabric in place. Basting is usually done to prepare the fabric for the next step in the project instructions. You don't need to backstitch when basting.

Casing

A fabric tunnel or sleeve for inserting elastic or a drawstring.

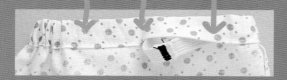

Fat quarter

A piece of fabric that measures approximately 18″ × 20″. You can buy these premeasured and cut at most fabric stores. A lot of the projects in this book need only a fat quarter of fabric.

Finger-press

To press seams open, or to press creases in the fabric, using your fingers instead of an iron.

Inseam

The inside seam of a pant leg.

Notches

Markings on the cutting line of a pattern piece. Cut around these triangles and notch shapes when cutting the fabric out.

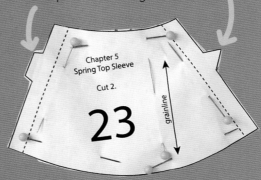

Chapter 5
Spring Top Sleeve

Cut 2.

23

grainline

Pinking shears

Scissors that make a zigzag cut (see page 11). Using pinking shears to cut your fabric out will stop the fabric from unraveling.

You can also use pinking shears after you sew a seam so you don't need to finish the raw edges of the seam allowance.

Pivot

To sew a corner or curve by leaving the needle down in the fabric, lifting the presser foot, and turning the fabric.

Pleats

Tiny folds sewn into the fabric or sewing project.

Right side of fabric

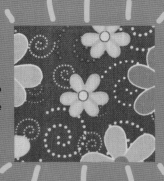

The pretty side— the side you want to show on the outside of your project.

Right sides together

When you sew two pieces of fabric together, you usually put the right sides together. The right sides are facing each other on the inside, and the wrong sides of the fabric are on the outside.

Seam

Sewing two pieces of fabric together forms a seam.

Seam allowance

The distance from the raw edge of the fabric to the stitching line.

Selvage

The finished edge of fabric that runs lengthwise.

Wrong sides together

The wrong sides of the fabric face each other.

Straight stitch

Sewing a straight line of stitches.

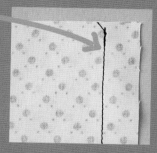

Zigzag stitch

In this stitch, the sewing machine needle moves from side to side, creating a wide stitch. You can change the width to sew either a narrow zigzag stitching line or a wide zigzag stitching line.

Wrong side of fabric

The dull side or the side you don't want to show on the outside of your project.

tip

When sewing with fabrics that do not have obvious right and wrong sides (like solid fabrics), using a tailor's chalk to mark the wrong side of each pattern piece after cutting will help you keep the pieces straight when sewing up the project.

2 On the Go

Simple Miniskirt
page 38

Simple Top
page 41

Flounce Skirt
page 44

Messenger Bag
page 48

Simple Miniskirt

back

What You'll Need

✕ Fat quarter (18″ × 20″) or ¼ yard of fabric

✕ 4½″ of ½″- or ¾″- wide hook-and-loop tape

✕ Pattern pieces 1 Front and 2 Back

✕ Your sewing basket (page 8)

What You'll Learn

✕ Using a pattern (page 14)

✕ Sewing seams (page 22)

✕ Making a double-folded hem (page 27)

✕ Sewing hook-and-loop tape (page 33)

Making the Miniskirt

Sew with a ¼″ seam allowance unless the instructions tell you otherwise.

step 1

Cut out the paper pattern pieces on pattern pullout page P1 (see Using a Pattern, page 14).

step 2

Fold your fabric with wrong sides together. Pin the pattern pieces onto your fabric, placing the Front piece on the fold. Cut the fabric on the solid lines of the pattern pieces (see Pinning the Pattern Pieces to the Fabric and Cutting Them Out, page 15).

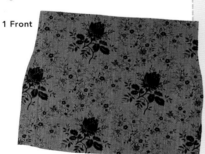

1 Front

2 Back

2 Back

step 3

Place the back pieces on top of the front piece, with right sides together. Pin the sides together. Using a ¼″ seam allowance, sew the side seams with a straight stitch (see Sewing Seams, page 22).

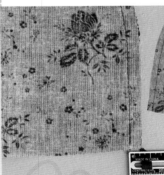

tip

Pinning the section you will be sewing helps to keep the fabric edges together while you sew.

step 4

Fold the top edge over ⅜″ to the inside of the skirt. Press the fold with an iron. Sew across the top edge with a straight stitch ¼″ from the folded edge.

step 5

Hem the bottom edge with a ½″ double-folded hem (see Making a Double-Folded Hem, page 27).

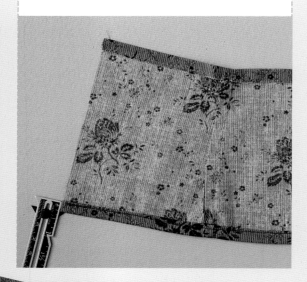

step 6

Sew the hook-and-loop tape back closure (see Sewing Hook-and-Loop Tape, page 33).

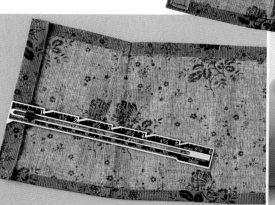

Simple Top

back

Making the Simple Top

Sew with a ¼″ seam allowance unless the instructions tell you otherwise.

step 1

Cut out the paper pattern pieces on pattern pullout page P1 (see Using a Pattern, page 14). Fold your fabric wrong sides together. Pin the pattern pieces onto your fabric, placing the Front piece on the fold. Cut the fabric on the solid lines of the pattern pieces (see Pinning the Pattern Pieces to the Fabric and Cutting them Out, page 15).

step 2

Place the back pieces on top of the front piece, with right sides together. Pin together at the shoulders, making sure the raw edges are even. Using a ¼″ seam allowance, sew across the shoulders with a straight stitch (see Sewing Seams, page 22).

Press the seams open using an iron or by finger-pressing (see Pressing Seam Allowances, page 26).

step 3

Fold the sleeve ends over toward the wrong side of the fabric ¼″ and press to keep them folded. Sew across the sleeves using a straight stitch.

step 4

Fold the neckline toward the inside ¼″ and finger-press. Sew the neckline using a straight stitch.

tip

The fabric is not going to stay folded easily while you sew the neckline. You'll need to sew slowly and stop to adjust the fabric as you sew, especially when sewing across the shoulder seams. Remember to keep the needle all the way down in the fabric when you adjust the fabric.

step 5

Place the front and back pieces with right sides together. Pin together at the sides, keeping the edges matched up. Using a ¼″ seam allowance, sew down the sides to the bottom edge using a straight stitch.

step 6

Fold the bottom edge toward the inside ⅝″ and press it. Sew across the bottom edge to hem the shirt, using a straight stitch.

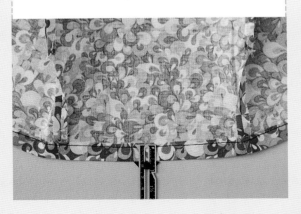

step 7

Sew the hook-and-loop tape back closure (see Sewing Hook-and-Loop Tape, page 33).

Flounce Skirt

Sewing level
⁕⁕

back

Sew in Style—Make Your Own Doll Clothes

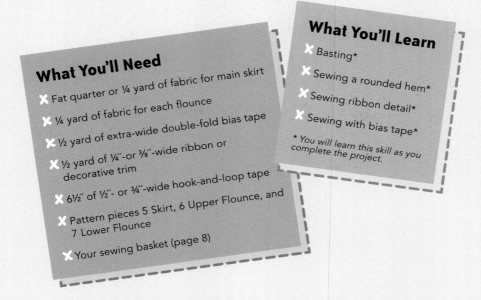

What You'll Need

- Fat quarter or ¼ yard of fabric for main skirt
- ¼ yard of fabric for each flounce
- ½ yard of extra-wide double-fold bias tape
- ½ yard of ¼"- or ⅜"-wide ribbon or decorative trim
- 6½" of ½"- or ¾"-wide hook-and-loop tape
- Pattern pieces 5 Skirt, 6 Upper Flounce, and 7 Lower Flounce
- Your sewing basket (page 8)

What You'll Learn

- Basting*
- Sewing a rounded hem*
- Sewing ribbon detail*
- Sewing with bias tape*

* You will learn this skill as you complete the project.

Making the Flounce Skirt

Sew with a ¼" seam allowance unless the instructions tell you otherwise.

step 1

Cut out the paper pattern pieces on pattern pullout page P1 (see Using a Pattern, page 14). Fold your fabric wrong sides together. Pin the pattern pieces onto your fabric, placing all 3 pieces on the fold. Cut the fabric on the solid lines of the pattern pieces (see Pinning the Pattern Pieces to the Fabric and Cutting Them Out, page 15).

5 Skirt

6 Upper Flounce

7 Lower Flounce

step 2

Fold the bottom edges of each flounce piece ¼" toward the wrong side of the fabric and press. Sew across the bottom edge of each flounce, using a straight stitch to hem them (see Sewing and Clipping Curves for help sewing the curve, page 32).

tip

If you can't iron, then finger-press and sew slowly. Hand sewing the hems is another way to get it done!

step 3

Lay the lower flounce with the right side of the fabric facing up. Place the upper flounce piece on top of the lower flounce piece, so that both right sides of the fabrics are facing up. Keep the top edges matched up and pin the flounces together. Baste together along the top edge by sewing with long, straight stitches ¼˝ from the edge.

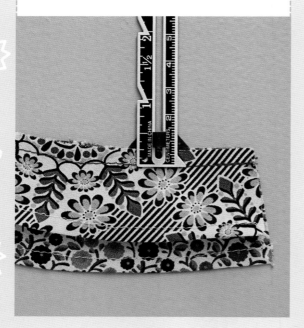

step 4

Pin the top edge of the flounces to the bottom edge of the main skirt piece, with right sides together. Using a ⅜˝ seam allowance, sew the flounces to the main skirt piece with a straight stitch (see Sewing Seams, page 22).

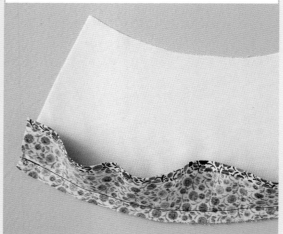

step 5

Wrap the bias tape around the top edge of the skirt, so that the skirt fabric is inside the bias tape, and pin it in place. Sew the bias tape onto the waist of the skirt close to the lower edge.

step 6

Press the seam allowances toward the top of the skirt. Pin the ribbon to the skirt just above the flounce. Sew the ribbon onto the main skirt piece. Sew slowly, stopping to adjust the ribbon when needed, as you did in Step 2. Trim any excess ribbon.

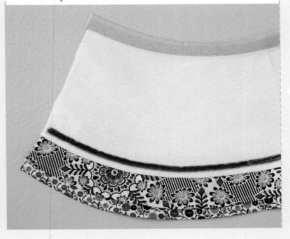

tip

You can also sew the bias tape onto the skirt using a zigzag stitch. Many people find this easier to do.

step 7

Sew the hook-and-loop tape back closure (see Sewing Hook-and-Loop Tape, page 33).

Messenger Bag

tip

For a quick and cute strap, use a 16″-long piece of pretty ½″-wide ribbon instead of fabric.

Making the Messenger Bag

Sew with a ¼″ seam allowance unless the instructions tell you otherwise.

step 1

Cut out the paper pattern piece on pattern pullout page P1 (see Using a Pattern, page 14). Fold your fabric with wrong sides together. Pin the pattern piece to your fabric, placing the piece on the fold. Cut the fabric on the solid lines of the pattern piece (see Pinning the Pattern Pieces to the Fabric and Cutting Them Out, page 15). Use the same pattern piece to cut out the lining piece, too. For the strap, cut a piece of fabric 2″ wide and 16″ long (see Cutting Fabric Pieces without Patterns, page 16).

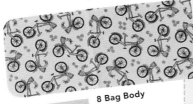

8 Bag Body

8 Bag Body Lining

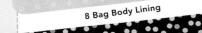

Strap

step 2

Place the bag and lining pieces with right sides together. Using a ⅜″ seam allowance, sew all the way around the bag, leaving about 2″ unsewn along a long edge.

Clip almost to the stitching line at curves and trim diagonally at corners. *Be careful not to cut any stitches.*

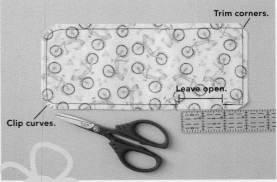

Trim corners.

Leave open.

Clip curves.

tip

Get more help with curves and corners in The Go-To Chapter (see Sewing and Trimming Corners, page 30, and Sewing and Clipping Curves, page 32).

step 3

Reach inside the opening and carefully pull the bag right side out. Poke and round the corners out with your fingers. Fold the fabric along the opening to the inside of the bag and press with an iron.

Sew the opening closed using a straight stitch.

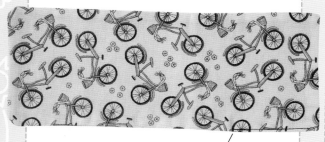

Sew closed.

step 4

Fold the bottom of the bag up to make the bag shape, making sure the exterior fabric is on the outside. Sew it in place along the sides.

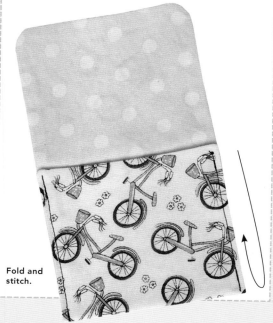

Fold and stitch.

step 5

Make the shoulder strap: Fold the edges of the fabric toward the center and press (#1). Fold in half lengthwise again and press (#2). Sew straight stitches along the edge (#3).

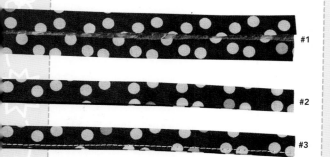

#1

#2

#3

step 6

Sew the strap in place by hand to the inside of the bag.

With her new bag and stylish clothes, your doll's definitely ready to go on an adventure!

3 Invited to a Party

Party Dress
page 52

Fashion Purse
page 56

**Ribbon and
Bead Bracelet**
page 59

Party Dress

Sewing level
✳✳

back

Making the Party Dress

Sew with a ¼″ seam allowance unless the instructions tell you otherwise.

step 1

Cut out the paper pattern pieces on pattern pullout page P1 (see Using a Pattern, page 14). Fold your fabric wrong sides together. Pin the pattern pieces to the fabric, placing the Skirt and Bodice Front pieces on the fold. Cut the fabric on the solid lines of the pattern pieces (see Pinning the Pattern Pieces to the Fabric and Cutting Them Out, page 15). Remember to use the Bodice Front and Bodice Back pattern pieces to cut out the lining pieces, too. Use a fabric marker to mark where the straps will go, on the right side of the bodice front.

Cut 2 pieces of ribbon 5″ long for the straps.

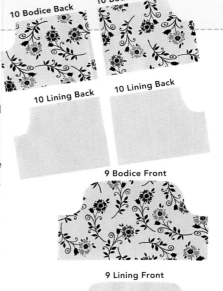

10 Bodice Back

10 Bodice Back

10 Bodice Back

10 Lining Back

10 Lining Back

9 Bodice Front

9 Lining Front

11 Skirt

step 2

Baste the straps to the right side of the bodice front, ¼˝ down from the top of the bodice (see Baste, page 34).

tip

If your ribbon has a right and a wrong side to it, then make sure to place the right side of the ribbon facing the right side of the fabric.

step 3

Place the bodice front and bodice back pieces right sides together, matching the side edges. Pin together at the sides. Using a ¼˝ seam allowance, sew the side seams.

Do the same thing for the lining front and lining back pieces.

Press all the side seams open (see Pressing Seam Allowances, page 26).

step 4

Pin the lining to the bodice along the top edge, with right sides together. Using a ¼˝ seam allowance, sew along the top edge.

Clip the curves and corners (see Sewing and Clipping Curves, page 32).

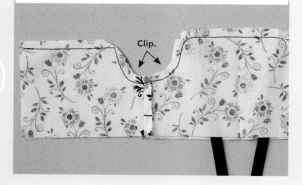

Clip.

step 5

Turn the bodice right side out. Poke out corners and smooth curves with your finger or corner-turning tool. Press with an iron.

Baste the bottom edge and center back edges of the bodice ¼˝ from the edges.

step 6

Fold the bottom edge of the skirt piece ¼″ toward the wrong side of the fabric and press with an iron. Sew across the bottom edge.

step 7

Pin the top edge of the skirt piece to the bottom edge of the bodice, with right sides together, matching the center back edges. Using a ⅜″ seam allowance, sew the skirt and bodice together. Finish the seam allowance with a zigzag stitch (see Finishing Seam Allowances, page 24).

Press the seam allowances toward the bodice.

step 8

Sew the hook-and-loop tape back closure (see Sewing Hook-and-Loop Tape, page 33).

step 9

Try the dress on your doll and carefully pin the straps in place on the wrong side of the bodice back. Take the dress off your doll and sew the straps in place.

Just tie a pretty ribbon on her dress for the sash.

Fashion Purse

Sewing level
*

Making the Purse

Sew with a ¼″ seam allowance unless the instructions tell you otherwise.

step 1

Cut out the paper pattern piece on pattern pullout page P2 (see Using a Pattern, page 14). Fold your fabric with wrong sides together. Cut the fabric on the solid lines of the pattern piece (see Pinning the Pattern Pieces to the Fabric and Cutting Them Out, page 15). Remember you'll need 2 pieces for the purse exterior and 2 pieces for the lining. They can be the same fabric or different.

12 Purse Lining   12 Purse Body

step 2

Pin a lining piece and an exterior piece right sides together. Using a ¼″ seam allowance, sew all around the sides and bottom. *Do not sew the top edge.* Repeat for the other lining and exterior pieces. Clip the curves (see Sewing and Clipping Curves, page 32).

Reach inside and turn both pieces right side out. Smooth out the curves with your finger or corner-turning tool. Fold the fabric along the opening to the inside and press it with an iron.

Sew the openings closed using a straight stitch.

Sew the strap to the lining side of 1 of the pieces.

Pin and sew the purse pieces together with the lining sides facing. *Do not sew the top closed.*

Your doll now has a great accessory to complement any outfit!

Ribbon and Bead Bracelet

Sewing level
*

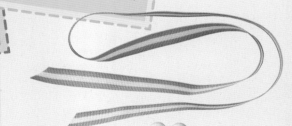

Making the Bracelet

step 1

Make a knot in the ribbon about 6″ from an end.

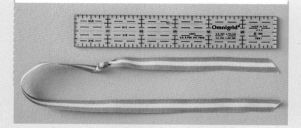

step 2

Fold the ribbon onto itself 3 times and sew it in place by poking a threaded needle through the center of the folded ribbon.

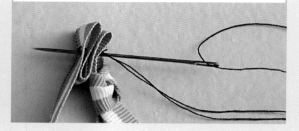

step 3

Add a bead onto the needle and fold the ribbon over the bead and needle. Add 2 more ribbon folds to the top and pull the needle through all the layers.

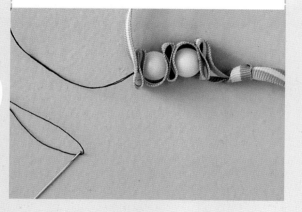

step 4

Keep folding the ribbon and adding beads until your bracelet is the length you want. End with a few folds of the ribbon.

step 5

When you're done sewing the ribbon and beads, make a few extra stitches through the last ribbon folds and tie a knot in your thread. Cut the extra thread.

Tie a knot in the ribbon and tie it onto your doll's wrist. Trim any extra ribbon.

This bracelet would make a great gift for a friend's doll.

4 It's a Sleepover

Camisole PJ Top
page 62

PJ Shorts
page 66

Sleep Mask
page 69

Sleeping Bag
page 71

Pillowcase
page 75

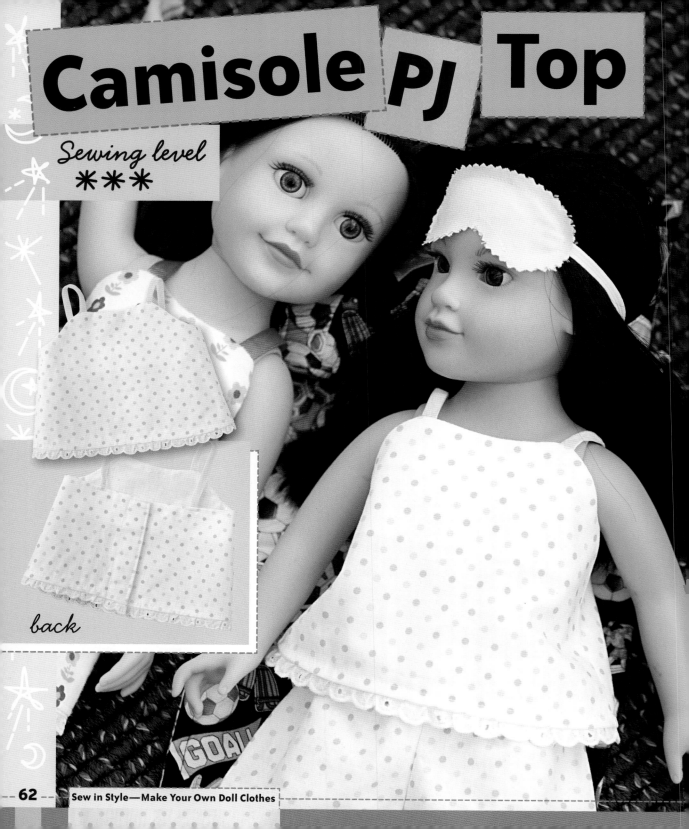

Camisole PJ Top

Sewing level ✱✱✱

back

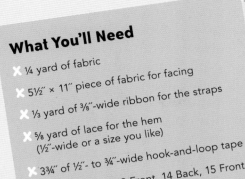

What You'll Need

- ✗ ¼ yard of fabric
- ✗ 5½″ × 11″ piece of fabric for facing
- ✗ ⅓ yard of ⅜″-wide ribbon for the straps
- ✗ ⅝ yard of lace for the hem (½″-wide or a size you like)
- ✗ 3¾″ of ½″- to ¾″-wide hook-and-loop tape
- ✗ Pattern pieces 13 Front, 14 Back, 15 Front Facing, and 16 Back Facing
- ✗ Your sewing basket (page 8)

What You'll Learn

- ✗ Sewing a sweetheart neckline*

* You will learn this skill as you complete the project.

Making the Camisole Top

Sew with a ¼″ seam allowance unless the instructions tell you otherwise.

step 1

Cut out the paper pattern pieces on pattern pullout page P2 (see Using a Pattern, page 14). Fold your fabric with wrong sides together. Pin the pattern pieces onto your fabric, placing the Front piece on the fold (when cutting facing pieces, place Front Facing piece on the fold). Cut the fabric on the solid lines of the pattern pieces (see Pinning the Pattern Pieces to the Fabric and Cutting Them Out, page 15). Use a fabric marker to mark where the straps will go.

step 2

Cut 2 pieces of ribbon, each 6″ long. Pin the ribbons to the right side of the bodice front and sew them in place.

14 Back

14 Back

13 Front

15 Front Facing

16 Back Facing

16 Back Facing

step 3

Place the front and back pieces right sides together, matching the side edges. Pin and sew the side seams.

Do the same thing to the front and back facing pieces. Press all 4 side seams open.

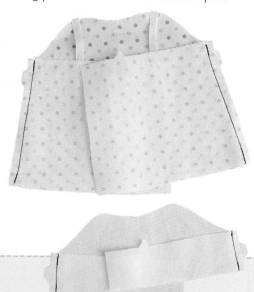

step 4

Place the lining and the camisole right sides together, matching the top edges. Pin along the top edge. Using a ¼˝ seam allowance, sew across the top.

Clip the curves, *but do not cut the stitches* (see Sewing and Clipping Curves, page 32).

tip

Careful! Slow stitching is needed to sew the curves on the camisole. A shorter stitch length on your sewing machine will help you to sew nicely rounded curves.

step 5

Turn the camisole right side out and use your fingers to smooth out the curves. Press the top edge with an iron.

step 6

Pin the lace to the bottom edge on the right side of the camisole. Sew it in place. Trim any excess lace.

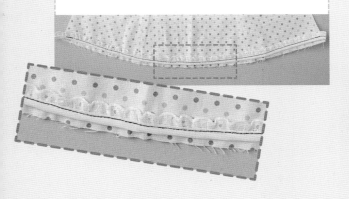

step 7

Fold and press the bottom edge toward the inside of the camisole, so that the lace now peeks out along the bottom. Sew just above the fold through both layers of fabric and the lace to hem the camisole.

Baste the center back opening ¼″ from the edge (see Basting, page 54)

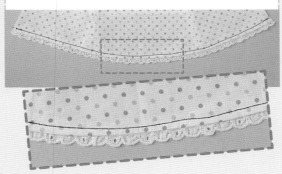

step 8

Sew the hook-and-loop tape back closure (see Sewing Hook-and-Loop Tape, page 33).

step 9

Put the camisole on your doll and adjust the straps to fit. Pin the straps in place on the wrong side of the back. Remove the camisole from your doll and sew the straps in place.

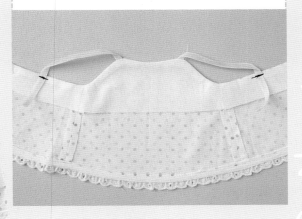

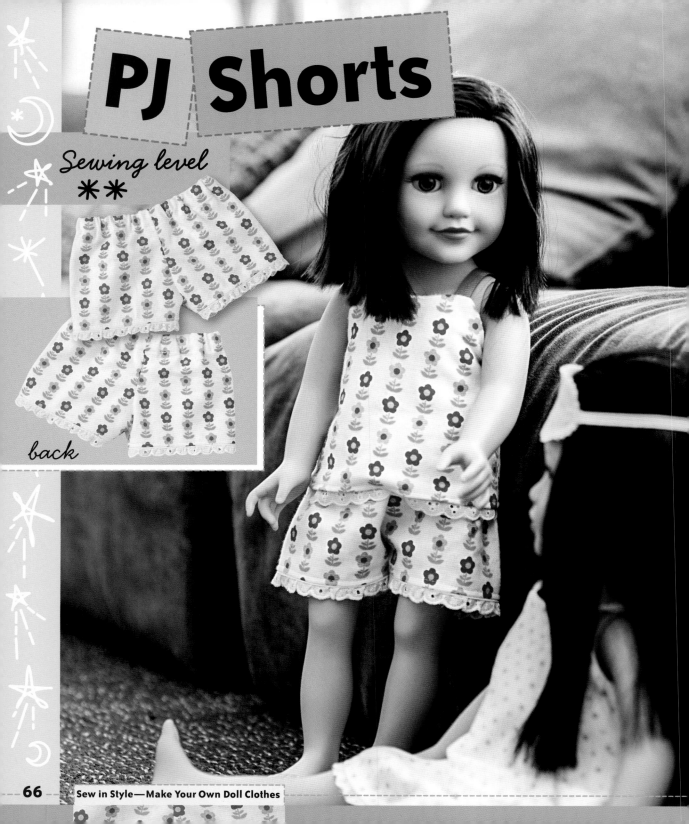

PJ Shorts

Sewing level
**

back

Sew in Style—Make Your Own Doll Clothes

Making the PJ Shorts

Sew with a ¼″ seam allowance unless the instructions tell you otherwise.

step 1

Cut out the pattern piece on pattern pullout page P2 (see Using a Pattern, page 14). Fold your fabric wrong sides together. Pin the pattern piece onto your fabric, placing it on the fold. Cut the fabric on the solid line of the pattern piece. Remove the pins from the fabric and repeat for the second leg (see Pinning the Pattern Pieces to the Fabric and Cutting Them Out, page 15).

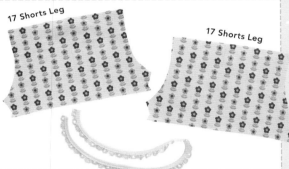

step 2

Pin the lace to the bottom edge of the shorts, with right sides together. Sew it in place. Trim any excess lace.

step 3

Fold the bottom edge toward the wrong side of the fabric and press. Sew across the bottom edge, just above the fold, through both layers of the fabric and the lace.

step 4

Fold both of the leg pieces in half, with right sides together. Pin and sew the inseams.

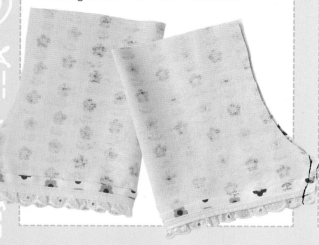

step 5

Turn a leg piece right side out and place it inside the other leg piece, matching the edges. The fabrics should be *right sides together*. Pin along the center front, crotch, and center back sections.

Sew the crotch seam using a ¼″ seam allowance. You will need to sew slowly and adjust the fabric occasionally, because it is a curved area.

step 6

Make the waistband casing and insert the elastic (see Sewing a Casing for an Elastic Waistband or Drawstring, page 28).

1. Make the casing and be sure to leave a 1½″ opening for the elastic.

2. Insert the elastic.

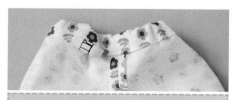

3. Pin and sew the ends of the elastic together.

4. Sew the opening closed.

Sleep Mask

Making the Sleep Mask

Sew with a ¼″ seam allowance unless the instructions tell you otherwise.

step 1

Cut out the paper pattern piece on pattern pullout page P2 (see Using a Pattern, page 14). Fold your fabric wrong sides together. Pin the pattern piece to your fabric. Using pinking shears, cut the fabric just to the outside of the solid lines of the pattern piece (see Pinning the Pattern Pieces to the Fabric and Cutting Them Out, page 15).

18 Mask **18 Mask**

step 2

Sew the elastic to the wrong side of a mask piece, so the cut ends are facing the middle of the mask. Make sure the elastic is not twisted.

step 3

Place the mask pieces wrong sides together, matching the edges. Sew all the way around.

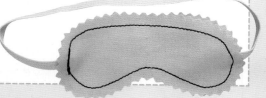

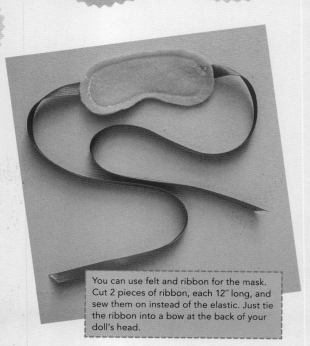

You can use felt and ribbon for the mask. Cut 2 pieces of ribbon, each 12″ long, and sew them on instead of the elastic. Just tie the ribbon into a bow at the back of your doll's head.

Sleeping Bag

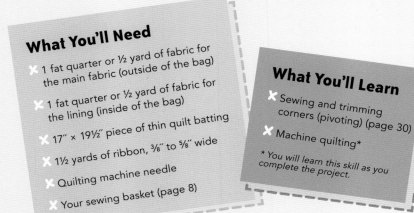

What You'll Need

✘ 1 fat quarter or ½ yard of fabric for the main fabric (outside of the bag)

✘ 1 fat quarter or ½ yard of fabric for the lining (inside of the bag)

✘ 17″ × 19½″ piece of thin quilt batting

✘ 1½ yards of ribbon, ⅜″ to ⅝″ wide

✘ Quilting machine needle

✘ Your sewing basket (page 8)

What You'll Learn

✘ Sewing and trimming corners (pivoting) (page 30)

✘ Machine quilting*

* You will learn this skill as you complete the project.

Making the Sleeping Bag

Sew with a ¼″ seam allowance unless the instructions tell you otherwise.

step 1

Cut out 2 pieces of fabric 17″ × 19½″: 1 is for the outside of the sleeping bag and 1 is for the lining (see Cutting Fabric Pieces without Patterns, page 16).

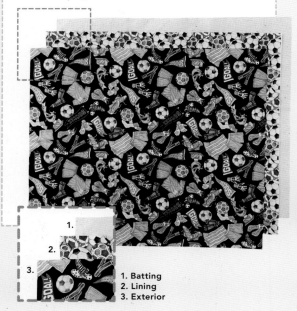

1. Batting
2. Lining
3. Exterior

step 2

Lay out the piece of batting and smooth out any wrinkles. Place the lining fabric on top of the batting, right side up. Place the exterior fabric on top of the lining fabric, right side down. Pin all 3 layers together. Your fabrics should be right sides together.

step 3

With the batting layer on top, sew all the way around the pinned-together layers using a ½″ seam allowance. *Leave 7″ unsewn* along a 19½″ side, beginning 1″ from the corner. Clip the corners (see Sewing and Trimming Corners, page 30).

Reach inside and carefully pull the bag right side out. With a corner-turning tool, reach inside and gently poke out the corners.

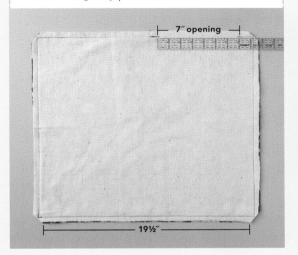

step 4

Fold the edges of the opening to the inside of the bag and press the opening. Press the rest of the bag.

Cut 2 ribbons, each 26″ long. Fold the ribbons in half and pin the folded part to the inside of the opening. Place the ribbons 1″ and 3″ from the corner.

Sew the opening closed, sewing the ribbons in place at the same time.

step 5

Use a ruler and fabric marker (or chalk) to draw vertical stitching lines about 2″ apart on the lining side of the bag across the shorter dimension.

Sew on these lines with long, straight stitches. This gives your bag a lofty, quilted look.

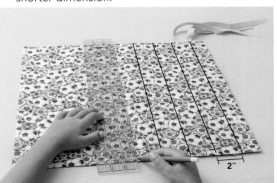

step 6

Fold the bag in half widthwise (the shorter direction), with lining sides facing. Place a pin along the open side 7˝ down from the top edge. Pin the rest of that side and the bottom edge. Sew the bag together where you've pinned, using a long stitch length.

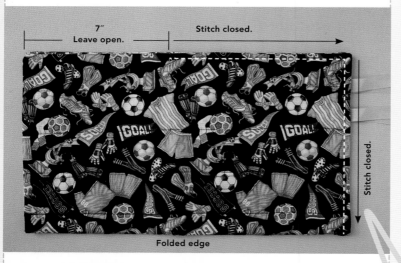

7˝
Leave open.

Stitch closed.

Stitch closed.

Folded edge

Folding the Sleeping Bag

To pack up your doll's sleeping bag, fold it in half lengthwise.

tip

Use Fray Check on the ribbon ends to keep them from unraveling.

Begin rolling from the top edge, and roll all the way to the bottom edge

Wrap the ribbons around the rolled bag and tie into bows.

Pillowcase

Sewing level
∗

Making the Pillowcase

Sew with a ¼" seam allowance unless the instructions tell you otherwise.

step 1

Use a ruler and fabric marker to measure and cut out the fabric pieces (see Cutting Fabric Pieces without Patterns, page 16).

step 2

Fold the cuff piece in half lengthwise, with wrong sides together. Press the fold with an iron.

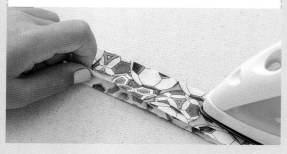

step 3

Pin the cuff to the right side of the main fabric piece. The folded edge of the cuff should be toward the center of the main piece. Sew together using a ⅜" seam allowance (see Sewing Seams, page 22).

Finish the seam allowance (see Finishing Seam Allowances, page 24).

Press the seam allowance toward the main fabric.

step 4

Fold the fabric in half, with right sides together. Pin the side and bottom seams, and sew using a ½" seam allowance, pivoting at the corners. Finish the seam allowances.

Turn the pillowcase right side out and gently poke the corners out.

tip

Consider making a pillow for your new pillowcase. Use a 6" × 12" piece of scrap fabric, fold it in half, and sew around 2 sides. Turn right side out. Stuff with fabric or batting scraps. Sew up the last side.

5 Hanging Out with Friends

Cuffed Shorts
page 78

Spring Top
page 81

Long-Sleeve Raglan T-Shirt
page 85

Headband
page 88

Yoga Pants
page 90

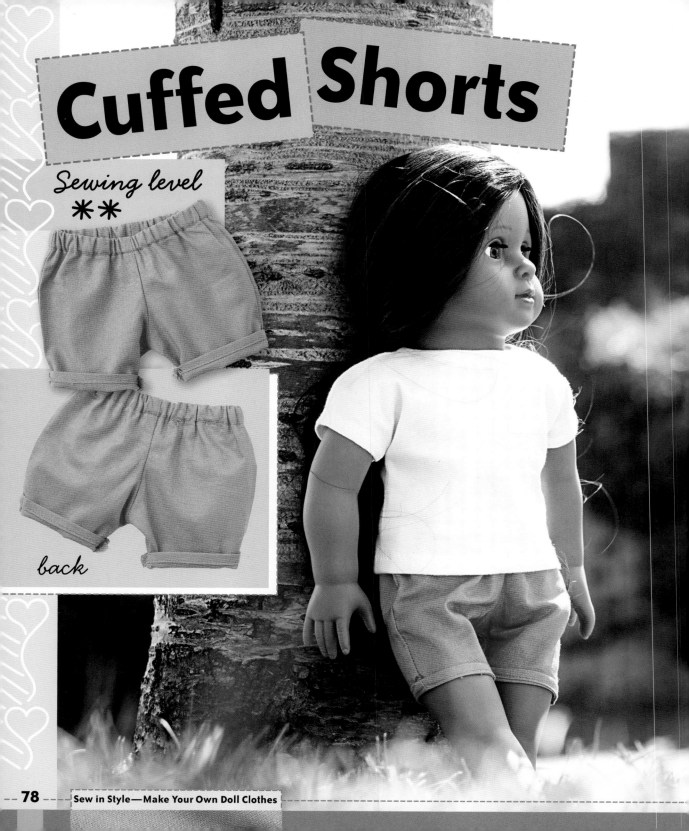

Cuffed Shorts

Sewing level
**

back

Making the Cuffed Shorts

Sew with a ¼" seam allowance unless the instructions tell you otherwise.

step 1

Cut out the paper pattern pieces on pattern pullout page P2 (see Using a Pattern, page 14). Fold your fabric wrong sides together. Pin the pattern pieces onto your fabric. Cut the fabric on the solid lines of the pattern pieces (see Pinning the Pattern Pieces to the Fabric and Cutting Them Out, page 15).

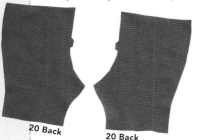

20 Back   20 Back

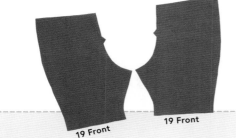

19 Front   19 Front

step 2

With right sides together, pin the front pieces to the back pieces along the sides. Then sew the side seams using a ¼" seam allowance.

Finish the seam allowances with a zigzag stitch (see Finishing Seam Allowances, page 24). Press the seam allowances toward the back.

step 3

Hem the shorts with a ⅝" double-folded hem (see Making a Double-Folded Hem, page 27).

step 4

Place the 2 pieces right sides together, matching the center front notches and the center back notches.

Pin and sew the center front edges together using a ¼″ seam allowance. Finish the seam allowances. Do the same thing for the center back.

step 5

Make a casing for the elastic waistband (see Sewing a Casing for an Elastic Waistband or Drawstring, page 28). Remember to leave a 2″ opening for inserting the elastic in Step 7.

step 6

Fold the shorts so the side seams are at the sides. Pin the inside of the legs right sides together, keeping the hems even. Sew the inseams with a ¼″ seam allowance. Finish the seam allowances (see Finishing Seam Allowances, page 24).

step 7

Insert the elastic and sew the opening closed.

Fold up the hems to make a cuff.

Spring Top

back

Making the Spring Top

Sew with a ¼″ seam allowance unless the instructions tell you otherwise.

step 1

Cut out the paper pattern pieces, cutting around the notches, on pattern pullout page P2 (see Using a Pattern, page 14). Fold your fabric wrong sides together. Pin the pattern pieces onto your fabric, placing the Front piece on the fold. Cut the fabric on the solid lines of the pattern pieces (see Pinning the Pattern Pieces to the Fabric and Cutting Them Out, page 15).

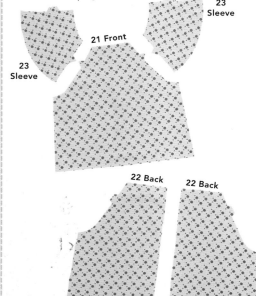

step 2

Note: If using optional trim, go to page 84. Fold the lower edge of the sleeves over ¼″ to the wrong side and press. Sew across the lower edge.

step 3

Pin the sleeve pieces to the back pieces, with right sides together, matching notches.

Sew the sleeves to the back pieces using a ¼″ seam allowance. Continue sewing past where the sleeves end, all the way down the arm opening to the side edge. This stitching will help you fold and press the arm opening more easily.

step 4

Sew the sleeves to the front piece in the same way you sewed the sleeves to the back pieces.

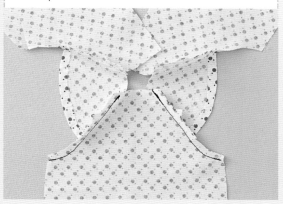

step 5

Press the seam allowances of the sleeves toward the front and the back. Continue pressing the arm openings toward the wrong side of the fabric. Finish the seam allowance and the folded edge of the arm openings.

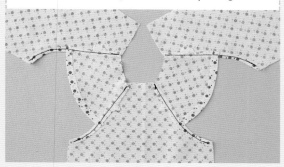

step 6

Fold the neckline ¼″ toward the wrong side of the fabric and press with an iron. Sew the neckline with a short straight stitch, stopping to adjust the fabric as you sew.

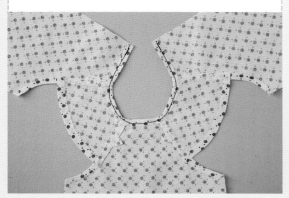

step 7

Pin and sew the side seams, with right sides together, using a ¼″ seam allowance.

step 8

Hem the bottom edge with a ½" double-folded hem (see Making a Double-Folded Hem, page 27).

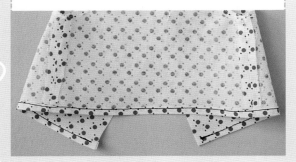

step 9

Sew the hook-and-loop tape back closure (see Sewing Hook-and-Loop Tape, page 33).

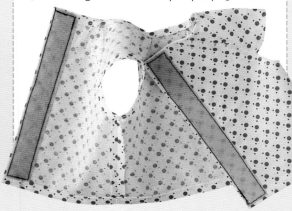

Adding Optional Ruffle Trim to the Sleeves

step 1

Pin the ruffle trim to the sleeves with right sides together.

step 2

Sew the trim to the sleeves.

step 3

Fold the sleeve ends toward the wrong side and press with an iron. Sew across the folded edge.

Continue with Step 3 of Making the Spring Top (page 82) to finish sewing the top.

Long-Sleeve Raglan T-Shirt

Sewing level
**

back

Making the Raglan T-Shirt

Sew with a ¼" seam allowance unless the instructions tell you otherwise.

step 1

Cut out the paper pattern pieces on pattern pullout pages P2 and P3 (see Using a Pattern, page 14). Fold your fabric with wrong sides together. Pin the pattern pieces onto your fabric, placing the Front piece on the fold. Cut the fabric on the solid lines of the pattern pieces (see Pinning the Pattern Pieces to the Fabric and Cutting Them Out, page 15).

26 Sleeve

26 Sleeve

24 Front

25 Back

25 Back

step 2

Fold the bottom edge of the sleeves ⅜" toward the wrong side and press with an iron. Sew across the folded edge with a wide zigzag stitch.

step 3

Pin the sleeves to the back pieces with right sides together, matching notches. Sew the sleeves to the back pieces using a ¼" seam allowance and a narrow zigzag stitch.

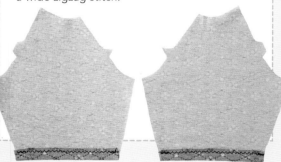

tip

Sewing with knits:

- ■ Use a stretch needle.
- ■ Use a narrow zigzag stitch for seams.
- ■ Use a wide zigzag stitch for hems and neckline.

step 4

Pin the sleeves to the front piece with right sides together, matching triangle notches. Sew the sleeves to the front using a ¼″ seam allowance and a narrow zigzag stitch.

step 5

Fold the neckline over ¼″ toward the inside of the shirt and press. Also press the sleeve seam allowances open, as shown below. Sew the neckline with a zigzag stitch.

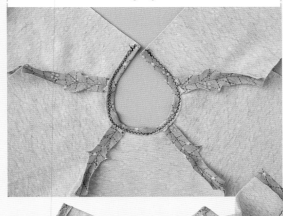

step 6

Pin the sides, with right sides together. Using a ¼″ seam allowance, sew the side seams with a narrow zigzag stitch, starting at the sleeve hem and sewing all the way to the bottom of the shirt.

step 7

Fold the bottom edge of the shirt ⅜″ toward the inside of the shirt and press. Sew the bottom edge with a wide zigzag stitch.

step 8

Sew the hook-and-loop tape back closure (see Sewing Hook-and-Loop Tape, page 33).

Headband

Sewing level
*

Making the Headband

Sew with a ¼″ seam allowance unless the instructions tell you otherwise.

step 1

Cut a piece of fabric 3½″ × 11½″ (see Cutting Fabric Pieces without Patterns, page 16).

step 2

Fold the headband in half lengthwise, with right sides together, and place pins 2″ from each end. Using a ⅜″ seam allowance, sew between the pins with a narrow zigzag stitch.

step 3

Turn it right side out. It's kind of like pulling a sleeve right side out. Reach into the tube and pull a little at a time, until it is turned completely right side out.

step 4

Open up the 2 ends and place them right sides together. Using a ¼″ seam allowance, sew along the edge with a narrow zigzag stitch.

step 5

Fold the edges of the opening to the inside and press. Sew the opening closed with a narrow zigzag stitch.

tip

You can also make this headband for yourself. Measure around your head and cut a piece of stretch knit fabric that is 4″ wide and 3″ shorter than your head measurement. Sew it just as you would for your doll. These make fun gifts to give to your friends or would be a fun project to sew with your friends.

Yoga Pants

back

Making the Yoga Pants

Sew with a ¼″ seam allowance unless the instructions tell you otherwise.

step 1

Cut out the paper pattern pieces on pattern pullout page P2 (see Using a Pattern, page 14). Fold your fabric with wrong sides together. Pin the pattern pieces onto your fabric. Cut the fabric on the solid lines of the pattern pieces (see Pinning the Pattern Pieces to the Fabric and Cutting Them Out, page 15).

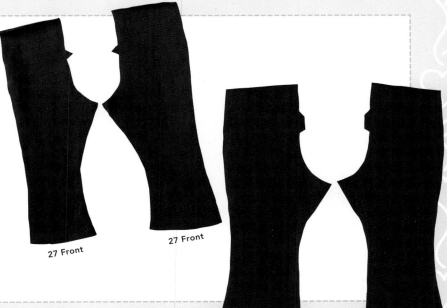

27 Front   27 Front

28 Back   28 Back

step 2

Pin the front pieces at the center front with right sides together, matching notches. Sew the center front using a ¼″ seam allowance and a narrow zigzag stitch. Do the same thing for the center back seam.

step 3

With right sides together, pin the front to the back at the sides. Using a ¼˝ seam allowance, sew the side seams with a narrow zigzag stitch.

step 4

Fold the bottom edge of the pant legs ⅜˝ toward the wrong side and press. Sew across the bottom edge with a narrow zigzag stitch.

step 5

Pin the inseams with right sides together. Sew the inseams with a narrow zigzag stitch (see Sewing Seams, page 22).

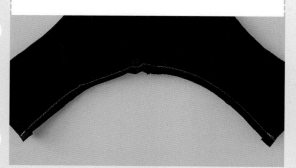

step 6

Fold the top edge at the waist 1˝ toward the wrong side of the fabric and press. Sew all the way around with a narrow zigzag stitch, close to the raw edge.

Fold the waistband over ⅝˝ toward the outside while wearing.

6 School Days

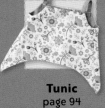

Tunic
page 94

Fitted Tee
page 98

**Skinny Jeans
or Pants**
page 101

Pleated Skirt
page 104

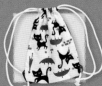

**Drawstring
Backpack**
page 107

Tunic

Sewing level
✳✳½

back

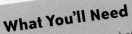

What You'll Need

✗ Fat quarter or ¼ yard of fabric for top

✗ 10″ × 10″ piece of fabric for the lining

✗ 1¼″ × 10″ piece of fabric for straps

✗ 5″ of ½″- to ¾″-wide hook-and-loop tape

✗ Pattern pieces 29 Front, 30 Back, 31 Front Lining, and 32 Back Lining

✗ Your sewing basket (page 8)

What You'll Learn

✗ Sewing spaghetti straps*

✗ Sewing a lined bodice*

✗ Sewing a curved hem*

You will learn this skill as you complete the project.

Making the Tunic

Sew with a ¼″ seam allowance unless the instructions tell you otherwise.

step 1

Cut out the paper pattern pieces on pattern pullout pages P2 and P3 (see Using a Pattern, page 14). Fold your fabric with wrong sides together. Pin the pattern pieces onto your fabric, placing the Front piece (and Front Lining piece) on the fold. Cut the fabric on the solid lines of the pattern pieces (see Pinning the Pattern Pieces to the Fabric and Cutting Them Out, page 15). Cut out the 1¼″ × 10″ strap piece (see Cutting Fabric Pieces without Patterns, page 16).

29 Front   30 Back   30 Back

31 Front Lining   32 Back Lining   32 Back Lining

Strap

step 2

Fold the bottom edges of the tunic front and back pieces ¼″ toward the wrong side of the fabric and press. Sew across the bottom edges.

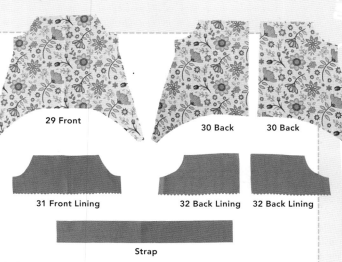

step 3

Use the 1¼″ × 10″ piece to make the straps (see Step 5 on page 50).

After the strap is sewn, cut it in half.

step 4

Sew the straps to the right side of the front piece.

tip

Sewing straps such as these and the messenger bag strap can be challenging. If you find it a bit too tricky and don't want to use ribbons, then you can try sewing them with a zigzag stitch. It's a bit easier to manage and looks great.

step 5

Sew the side seams of the lining pieces and the tunic pieces with right sides together using a ¼″ seam allowance (see Step 3 of the Party Dress project on page 54).

Finish the seam allowances with a zigzag stitch (see Finishing Seam Allowances, page 24).

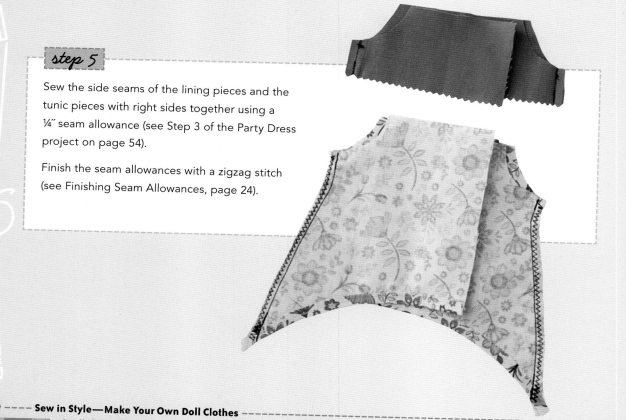

step 6

Pin the lining to the tunic with right sides together. Using a ¼˝ seam allowance, sew across the top edge.

Clip the curves and trim the corners (see Sewing and Trimming Corners, page 30).

step 7

Turn the tunic right side out and press (see Step 5 of the Party Dress project on page 54).

Finish the center back edges with a zigzag stitch.

step 8

Sew the hook-and-loop tape back closure (see Sewing Hook-and-Loop Tape, page 33).

step 9

Sew straps to the back (see Step 9 of the Party Dress project on page 55).

Fitted Tee

Sewing level
＊ ½

back

Making the Fitted Tee

Sew with a ¼˝ seam allowance unless the instructions tell you otherwise.

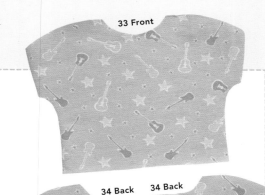

step 1

Cut out the paper pattern pieces on pattern pullout page P3 (see Using a Pattern, page 14). Fold your fabric with wrong sides together. Pin the pattern pieces onto your fabric, placing the Front piece on the fold. Cut the fabric on the solid lines of the pattern pieces (see Pinning the Pattern Pieces to the Fabric and Cutting Them Out, page 15).

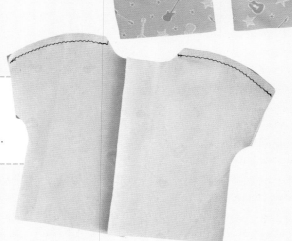

step 2

Pin the front to the back at the shoulders. Using a ¼˝ seam allowance, sew the shoulder seams with a narrow zigzag stitch.

step 3

Fold the sleeve openings ¼″ toward the wrong side of the fabric and press. Sew across the folded edge with a narrow zigzag stitch.

step 4

Fold the neckline ¼″ toward the inside and press. Sew the neckline using a narrow zigzag stitch.

step 5

With right sides together, pin the sides. Using a ¼″ seam allowance, sew the side seams with a narrow zigzag stitch.

step 6

Fold the bottom edge ⅜″ toward the inside and press. Sew the bottom edge with a wide zigzag stitch.

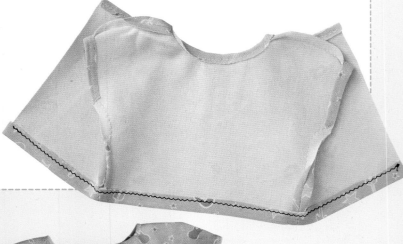

step 7

Sew the hook-and-loop tape back closure (see Sewing Hook-and-Loop Tape, page 33).

Skinny Jeans or Pants

Sewing level
✳✳½

back

Making the Skinny Jeans or Pants

Sew with a ¼″ seam allowance unless the instructions tell you otherwise.

step 1

Cut out the paper pattern pieces on pattern pullout page P3 (see Using a Pattern, page 14). Fold your fabric with wrong sides together. Pin the pattern pieces onto your fabric. Cut the fabric on the solid lines of the pattern pieces (see Pinning the Pattern Pieces to the Fabric and Cutting Them Out, page 15).

35 Front   35 Front

36 Back   36 Back

step 2

With right sides together, pin the front pieces to the back pieces along the sides. Using a ¼″ seam allowance, sew the side seams. Finish the seam allowances with a zigzag stitch (see Finishing Seam Allowances, page 24).

Optional Topstitching Detail: Press the seam allowances toward the back of each pant leg. Work with the right side facing up and sew close to the seam through all 3 layers, using a straight stitch.

step 3

Hem the pants with a ⅝″ double-folded hem (see Making a Double-Folded Hem, page 27).

step 4

Sew the center front and the center back seams (see Step 4 of Cuffed Shorts on page 80).

step 5

Make a casing along the waist, leaving an opening to insert the elastic in Step 7 (see Sewing a Casing for an Elastic Waistband or Drawstring, page 28).

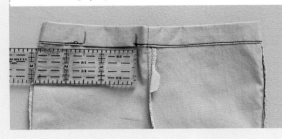

step 6

Place the leg pieces with right sides together. Using a ¼″ seam allowance, sew the inseams (see Step 6 of Cuffed Shorts on page 80).

step 7

Insert the elastic and sew the opening closed.

tip

Roll up the hems for a fun cropped-jeans look.

Pleated Skirt

Sewing level
**

back

Making the Pleated Skirt

Sew with a ¼″ seam allowance unless the instructions tell you otherwise.

step 1

Cut out the paper pattern pieces on pattern pullout page P3 (see Using a Pattern, page 14). Fold your fabric with wrong sides together. Pin the pattern pieces onto your fabric. Cut the fabric on the solid lines of the pattern pieces (see Pinning the Pattern Pieces to the Fabric and Cutting Them Out, page 15). Use a fabric marker to mark the pleat lines onto the front skirt piece.

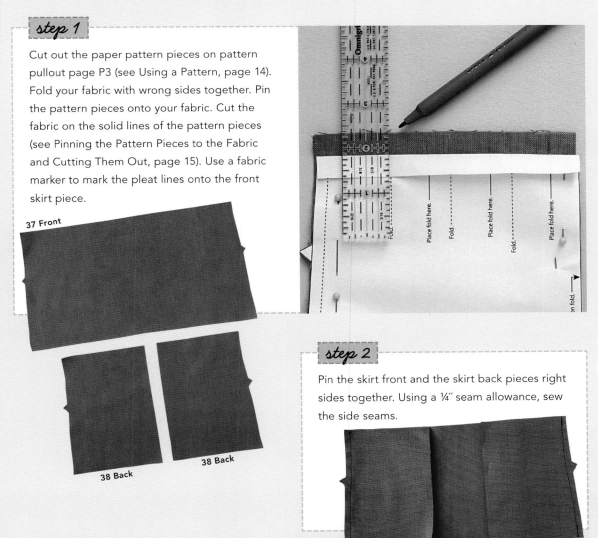

37 Front

38 Back   38 Back

step 2

Pin the skirt front and the skirt back pieces right sides together. Using a ¼″ seam allowance, sew the side seams.

step 3

Hem the bottom edge with a ½″ double-folded hem (see Making a Double-Folded Hem, page 27).

step 4

For each pleat, fold the fabric on the dotted line and place that fold on the solid line next to it, moving in the direction of the arrows. Press each pleat as you fold it (all the pleats should go toward the center). Pin them in place and baste by sewing long, straight stitches across the pleats, ¼″ from the top edge.

step 5

Fold the waist ⅜″ toward the inside of the skirt and press. Sew across the top edge.

step 6

Sew the hook-and-loop tape back closure (see Sewing Hook-and-Loop Tape, page 33).

tip

Remember to try the skirt on your doll before you sew the hook-and-loop tape. That way, it will fit your doll perfectly.

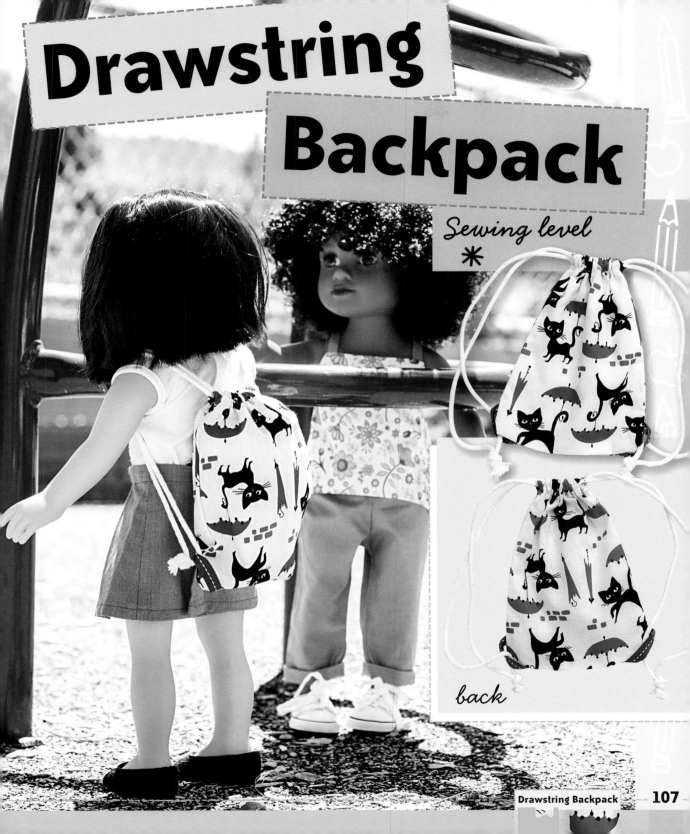

Drawstring
Backpack

Sewing level
*

back

tip

You can also make a backpack for yourself. Just start with fabric pieces 14″ × 18″. You'll need 2 pieces of cording, each 64″ long.

Making the Backpack

Sew with a ¼″ seam allowance unless the instructions tell you otherwise.

step 1

Using pinking shears, cut out the fabric pieces (see Cutting Fabric Pieces without Patterns, page 16).

step 2

Make a casing along the top edge of each piece (see Sewing a Casing for an Elastic Waistband or Drawstring, page 28).

step 3

Cut the ribbon in half. Pin the ribbons to the right side of a bag piece at the bottom corners, looped as shown, 1″ up and in from the corners. Sew them in place. Trim any extra ribbon.

step 4

Pin the bag pieces with right sides together, matching the top and bottom. Using a ½″ seam allowance, sew both sides and the bottom. *Do not sew the casing openings closed. Stop and start sewing just below the casings.*

step 5

Put a safety pin through the end of a piece of cording and feed it though the casing. When it reaches the other side, put it into the second casing and feed it through the other side, so that it comes back out on the same side that it went into.

Do the same thing for the second piece of cording—only this time, start and stop on the opposite side and go the opposite direction.

Each piece of cording should have both ends coming out on the same side. Put each piece of cording through the ribbon loop on its own side. Remove the safety pin and tie the ends of the cording together in a knot to form straps.

Pull on both cords to close the top of the backpack and make the handles long enough for your doll to wear her backpack.

final Thoughts

I hope you have as much fun creating doll clothes and accessories with this book as I have had designing the patterns and writing this book.

Now it's time to add your own touches and make the designs pop! There are many ways to change things up so the same pattern takes on many different looks. Here are just some of the ways.

Rock It

Use iron-on jewels to add some interesting detail to any of your designs.

Make It Graphic

Use rubber stamps and fabric paint to transform a basic tee into a cool graphic tee. Lightly brush a very thin layer of fabric paint onto the rubber stamp. Carefully press the stamp onto the fabric. I like to test on scrap fabric first. You may want to stamp on your fabric before sewing the tee, to make sure it's a look you like.

Ribbon, Lace, and Trim

Lace and trims are in no short supply out there. You can find some really great trendy ones to embellish with.

Add lace to any hem, or even to the necklines. Just sew it on, or follow the how-to on page 67 in Chapter 4.

Ribbons and trims can be sewn right onto the skirt, dress, or top. You can even use a contrasting thread and a zigzag stitch for some extra flair.

All designers brainstorm for new things to try. Some of those things turn into new fashion trends. The main idea here is to have fun trying new things.

Get Your Stitch On

You can use embroidery floss to "draw" designs on your projects. Use a fabric pen to draw a simple line drawing. Sew a running stitch or backstitch along the drawn lines. Using embroidery floss to sew a hem is also a great decorative touch. You could stitch X's or V's for a design. Play around with your own design ideas and get creative!

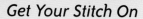

resources Guide

Sewing is less frustrating and much more fun when you have the proper tools. I encourage you to shop at your locally owned craft and fabric stores. They usually have really cute and unique fabrics and trims, as well as high-quality tools and notions. When I can't find something locally, I look online. Here are some of my favorite online sources.

For Fun Knit Fabrics

Many of the knits shown in the book came from a local fabric shop, The Rain Shed, but some came from pretty cool little online shops as well.

Print Knit Studio
printknitsstudio.com

SewZanne's
Check out her "Fabric-tionary"— it will help you understand the different types of fabric better.
sewzannesfabrics.com

The Fabric Fairy
thefabricfairy.com

Tools and Supplies
Dritz/Prym
Dritz makes a number of sewing tools and gadgets that make sewing much easier. Its Omnigrid rulers come in many useful sizes; the one I use most for sewing my doll projects is the 1″ × 12″ size. *dritz.com*

Havel's Sewing
Havel's makes 5½″ serrated embroidery/sewing scissors that work very well for cutting out small projects like doll clothes. These scissors are the perfect size for smaller hands, and the serrated edges help to hold the fabric in place as you cut. Havel's pinking shears are super easy to cut with as well.
havelssewing.com
blog.havelssewing.com

The Wooly Thread
I use Swedish tracing paper to trace all my patterns. I buy it from The Wooly Thread.
woolythread.com

Fabrics
Fabric comes in every color and a wide variety of designs to express every kind of personality.

Most of the projects shown in the book were made using woven fabrics, also known as quilting cottons. Many came from my local shops in town, Creative Crafts and Quiltwork Patches, but a good number also came from online sources. Here are a few of my favorites places to shop for fabric online. Some fabric companies have online blogs and share awesome sewing projects on them. Blogs are a great place to find some creative inspiration.

Dear Stella
dearstelladesign.com
dearstelladesign.com/blog

Etsy • *etsy.com*

Riley Blake Designs
rileyblakedesigns.com
rileyblakedesigns.com/blog

RJR Fabrics • *rjrfabrics.com*

about
the Author

Erin's favorites:

Animal: Rabbit

Book: *The Lion, the Witch, and the Wardrobe*

Card game: Set

Food: Crepes with butter and powdered sugar

Movie: *The Princess Bride*

Sport: Soccer

Video game: *Mario Kart: Double Dash!!* (for the Nintendo GameCube)

Erin first fell in love with sewing at age seven, when she attended a kids' sewing class at the Lucie Stern Community Center in Palo Alto, California. While growing up, she enjoyed sewing stuffed animals for friends and clothing for herself and, of course, for her dolls.

Erin holds a bachelor of science degree from Oregon State University and lives in the beautiful Willamette Valley, Oregon, with her husband, children, two cats, chinchilla, and house rabbit. She teaches sewing locally and is an active volunteer in her daughter's 4-H sewing group.

She is the designer and blogger behind Avery Lane Designs, an Etsy doll-clothing pattern shop.

Find Erin online:
etsy.com/shop/averylane

averylanesewing.com